STRANGERS

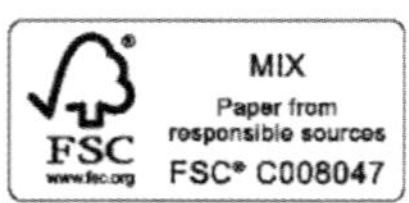
MIX
Paper from
responsible sources
FSC® C008047

STRANGERS

ISMAIL EINASHE

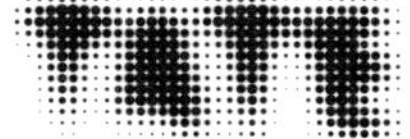

Director's Statement

'Look Again' is a bold new publishing programme from Tate Publishing and Tate Britain. In these books, we are providing a platform for some of the most exciting contemporary voices writing today to explore the national collection of British art in their own way, and reconnect art to our lives today. The books have been developed ahead of the rehang of Tate Britain's collection, which foregrounds many of the artworks discussed here. In this third set of books – *Death* by Sean Burns, *Strangers* by Ismail Einashe *Girlhood* by Claire Marie Healy, and *Faith* by Derek Owusu – we are offered unique perspectives on a wide range of artworks across British history, and encouraged to look closely, and to look again.

Alex Farquharson, Director, Tate Britain

In the summer of 1748, the British painter William Hogarth embarked on his second visit to France. On his return trip home via Calais, while sketching in the town, he was arrested by French police and held for a short time on suspicion of being a spy.

On his release, he set sail, relieved, for London. He quickly painted *O the Roast Beef of Old England* (*'The Gate of Calais'*) 1748.

This picture is named after a patriotic eighteenth-century song that lauded roast beef as symbolising British pride, uniqueness and superiority. Hogarth's painting is partly a Protestant satire of the Catholic Church, but it is also laden with a nationalistic and xenophobic aesthetic, rife with Gallophobia and

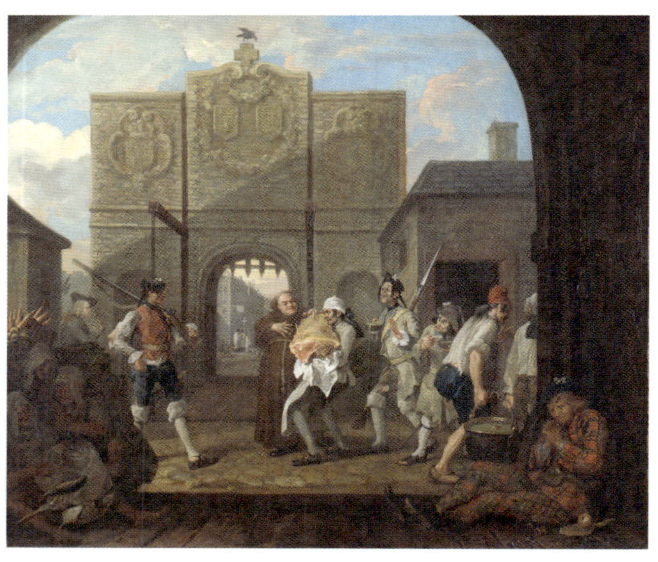

William Hogarth, *O The Roast Beef of Old England (The Gates of Calais)* 1748, oil paint on canvas, 78.8 x 94.5, Tate

anti-Jacobite sentiments. We see scraggy French soldiers eating bowls of measly-looking soup and gawking at the large cut of beef destined for the English Inn in Calais while a corpulent French friar eyes the meat with a devilish appetite. The rib of beef – elemental, sinewy and solid and red-blooded – is a thing of envy. The painting includes a self-portrait of Hogarth, who presents himself as an impartial observer documenting what he sees – except that his view is clearly not objective or unbiased. Instead, he is eager to showcase his unfavourable view of the French.

The centrality of Calais is vital to this work. The French town is the closest port to England, just twenty-one miles across the Channel from Dover, and marks the border between Britain and 'strangers' out there in the continent. Calais was English for two hundred years after being conquered in 1347 by Edward III; centuries on, Calais is still the literal 'Gate of Britain' to Europe and beyond, but it now boasts a large modern port, Eurostar rail services and a heavy flow of goods and passenger ferry traffic. A physical gate to non-British otherness, Calais is also a gateway to imagining otherness, and in this painting, in this liminal space between Englishness and otherness, Hogarth is intent on imposing an idea that the honest meat of Englishness is at threat from the perfidious other, be it French, Catholic or Scottish. Whatever possibilities exist beyond the gate, materially or in the imagination, are pre-laden with distaste.

Hogarth's picture reminds us that this border has, for centuries, been securitised to keep 'strangers', 'aliens' and 'foreigners' out from our green and pleasant island. Today, Calais is where migrants such as Afghanis, Eritreans, Iranians, Syrians, and Iraqis board small boats, scale security fences or climb on the backs of lorries bound for Britain. But these migrants are just the latest iteration of a flow of people across the English Channel that has shaped Britain's culture over the centuries, from the French Protestant Huguenots who escaped religious persecution in the 1680s to Jewish Europeans who arrived before the onset of the Second World War, to Kosovans who came in the late 1990s fleeing genocide in the Balkans.

For decades, the spectre of migrants crossing the Channel has fed a toxic anti-immigrant sentiment in the media and political space. However, the clouds over this body of water have darkened profoundly over the last few years. A handful of years after Britain watched with indifference the loss of migrant lives in the Mediterranean, the cold tides of the Channel now serve up their own deadly body count. The pictures of discarded life jackets and deflating dinghies once seen on the shores of Greece have been replaced by similar images on Kentish beaches. 'Stop the Boats' has become a mantra, while the ratcheting up of anti-immigrant rhetoric and violence has led to scenes of far-right mobs assembling at hotels to intimidate and attack the asylum seekers housed there.

Meanwhile, the current Home Secretary, Suella Braverman, speaks about her 'dream' of seeing a flight full of asylum seekers take off to Rwanda. In this Orwellian situation, a British politician, the daughter of migrants, is proud of her 'obsession' with sending vulnerable people to an authoritarian state infamous for its terrible human rights record. A photograph released from Braverman's March 2023 trip to inspect an empty migrant facility in Rwanda shows the Home Secretary laughing joyfully. The sad truth is that being a stranger yourself does not preclude one from prejudice and xenophobia.

'No one leaves home unless home is the mouth of a shark'

This book is not just about the intersection of art and migration but specifically about the idea of 'strangers'. By definition, strangers are not friends; a stranger is someone you don't know, whose foreignness or otherness may be a threat. A stranger can also be an 'intruder': someone not seen to belong to a group or who is kept from its activities. But a stranger can also be a guest or a visitor – someone we do not need to vilify or fear and who may require our assistance, compassion and empathy as fellow humans.

Although the words' migrant' and 'refugee' are used interchangeably in the media, they mean different things and fit differently into the notion of 'strangers'. Strictly defined, a migrant moves by choice, and a refugee is forced to flee their home because of war, persecution or violence. But describing people as refugees has become too politically charged, while the word remains too limited to sufficiently describe the scope and diversity of those on the move. Merely calling everyone on the move a refugee feeds our liberal biases and underscores problematic notions of who deserves asylum, protection and safe passage. When we think like this, we end up with a league table of migrants' suffering, with some more deserving than others – a Dickensian way to reduce the complex experiences of people on the move.

Likewise, we tend to view these strangers through a narrow binary, as either vulnerable victims or dangerous intruders, and to frame their personhood in terms of their labour or suffering. When we do that, we obscure their cultural capital and their ability to participate in art by and about them. This raises the question: Why do we tend to view migration through its economic, social or policy dimensions – but never through its artistic or cultural ones?

Today, we are dealing with complex factors regarding global migratory movements: conflict, climate change, and poverty. We have also seen the largest ever displaced population, with 100 million people displaced by war from Ukraine, Ethiopia, Syria and Afghanistan. We need a new way of looking at and thinking about immigration, which remains at the heart of the British predicament – one beyond the current problematising media and political lens. Here, art can tell us a lot about immigration that politics cannot: it can allow us to sidestep dehumanising language and problematic representations and offer us a deeper window into the emotional and human journey of the migrant. By connecting us, through empathy, to the plight of the displaced, art can allow us to move beyond our cultural confines into a shared non-verbal, visual language of human connections and understanding. What's more, art about migration does not need to be overtly political to allow us to sit with the stranger – it can be about everyday experiences such as food rituals, sensory layers, memory and feelings of home.

The Somali photographer Mustafa Saeed shot *Monument* 2014 just outside my city of birth, Hargeisa, in Somaliland. Part of Saeed's *Home and Me* series, the photograph captures the beauty of the Somali landscape. A traditional textile, the lined Al Hindi cloth, with its red, amber and maroon colours, is suspended in mid-air with an acacia tree in the background. These colour formations speak to the rich history of Somali artisanship. *Monument* also smells of home: the image is framed with a traditional Somali dabqaad (also known as girgir), an incense burner used to perfume the home or oneself. In this way, Saeed's work speaks to the sensuality of home, the feeling and the smell of being.

The Somali word 'buufis' means 'to blow' or 'to inflate', but for Somalis, the term conjures up the spiritual aspects of migrating or wanting to escape elsewhere. It speaks to that deep yearning for adventure and our hope for a bright future when we imagine our lives if we left for a bigger city or a more affluent country with better opportunities to earn and support our families. For me, 'buufis' is a concept which brings alive the act of migration. Crossing borders, scaling metal fences, and boarding dinghies are acts not only of survival but of the imagination.

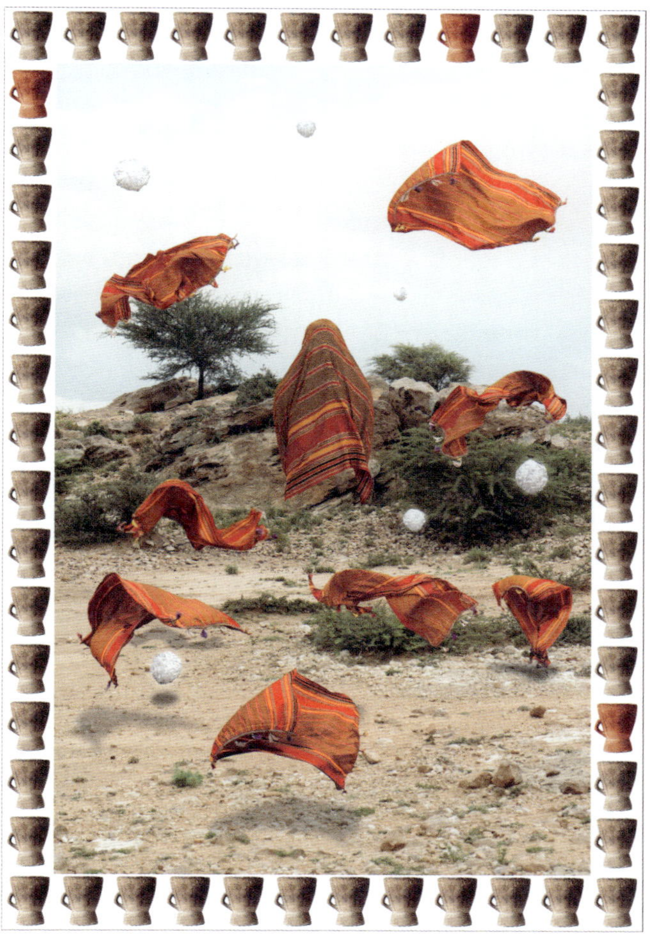

Mustafa Saeed, *Monument* 2014, lens based image, collage with other images made on the spot, 42 x 60

For no one chooses to give up the comforts of home, yet conflict forces people to make perilous journeys abroad. The British-Somali poet Warsan Shire movingly captured the pain of displacement in her poem 'Home' with the unforgettable line, 'no one leaves home unless home is the mouth of a shark'. I became a stranger because home spat me out when war forced my family to flee our home in Hargeisa for a refugee camp in Ethiopia – at the time, the largest of its kind anywhere in the world. I remember it as an unforgiving dusty expanse covered by a sea of white tents, full of desperation and disease. And so, despite my having long left the conflict behind, the shadow of Somalia's war still remains with me.

'Dignity has no nationality'

Tania Bruguera, the renowned Cuban performance artist, is known for her interventions in this space of art and migration. Bruguera centres the lived experience of migrants in her work, making it a powerful antidote to the cliché-heavy, problematising and dehumanising depictions we see of strangers elsewhere. In her socio-political project in Queens, New York, the *Immigrant Movement International* (2010–15), Bruguera meshed art and migration to engage with the issues faced by migrants and to see how these fit into broader social discourses.

Throughout her career, Bruguera has explored the ways in which control, oppression and violence are deployed against migrants. Her interventions have been about challenging the way the migrant experience is disregarded and ensuring that the migrant is not treated as an object merely to be understood through their utility (or lack thereof) in society. She has often said that 'dignity has no nationality'. Through installation, performances and a socially engaged art practice, Bruguera seeks to explain what art can usefully do in the face of the contemporary crises we face, particularly concerning the plight of the displaced. In 2003 she devised the concept of Arte Útil (useful art): art which engages with the socio-political to advance solutions to political issues.

In Bruguera's *Tatlin's Whisper #5* 2008, a performance in Tate Modern's Turbine Hall, two mounted policemen patrolled the gallery space, controlling the crowd via the same measures used by police at major public events. Bruguera's work plays with the idea of crowd control, showing how security methods deployed in a public context, such as a royal wedding, can have a different meaning if used during a political protest to disperse and detain demonstrators.

Bruguera offers a more profound commentary about the relationship between those who control and those who are controlled. The migrant's physical world is often managed through borders, detention centres and by traffickers; Bruguera's work speaks to the migrant's journey and the motion of the migrant body and mind through different states of control – whether at the Austrian border in 2015 during the so-called 'migrant crisis' or today on the US border, where similar crowd control methods are used to detain Latin American migrants.

In Francis Alÿs's twenty-channel video installation *The Nightwatch* 2004, a fox – released by the artist – moves through the National Portrait Gallery late one night, traversing galleries containing essential works of British art of the sixteenth, seventeenth and eighteenth centuries: an intruder trespassing the gilded cultural heart of London. The work is a meditation on being 'inside' and 'outside' – allowed in, yet not seen or welcomed. But by using the museum's many CCTV cameras to track the fox's progress, Alÿs also makes a powerful comment on the idea of strangers as interlopers and the mechanisms by which we can monitor the movements of such 'invaders'. In recent years, liberal states have built sophisticated surveillance systems, walls and vast border systems designed, they claim, to keep migrants out. Yet the same

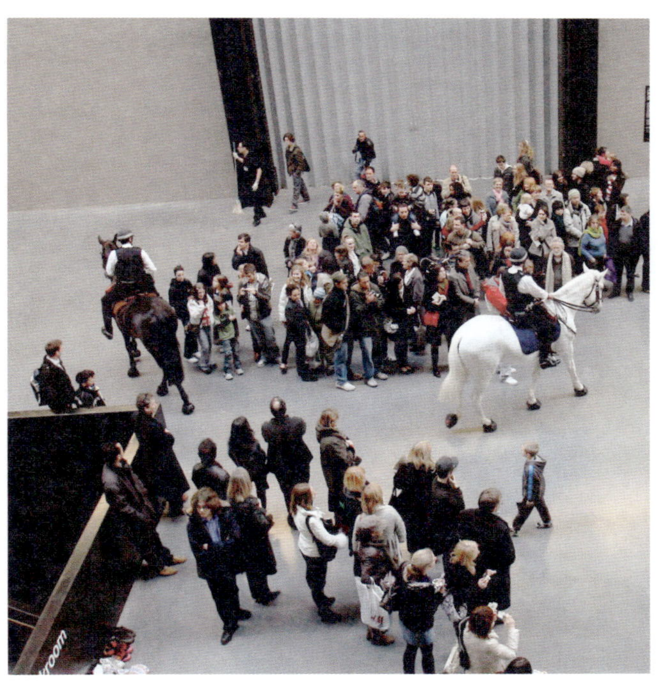

Tania Bruguera, *Tatlin's Whisper #5*, 2008, performance (two people and two horses

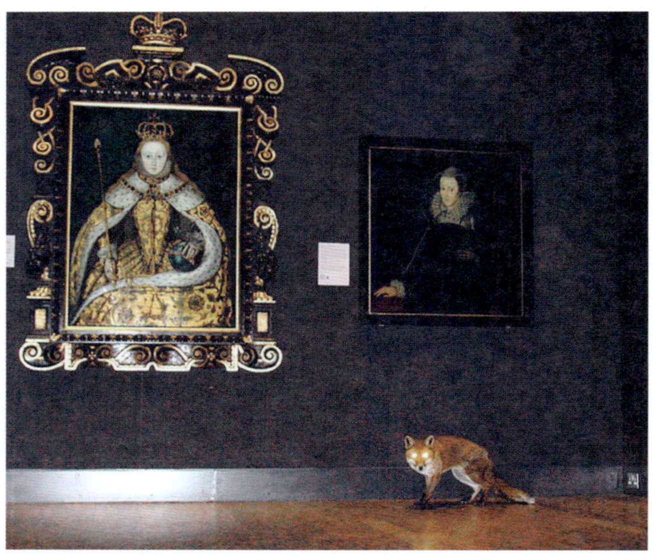

Francis Alÿs, *The Nightwatch* 2004, video, two maps, printed papers, seven drawings and book, duration nineteen minutes, 234 x 284 x 60, Tate

techniques can also limit the rights of the very citizens these states claim they are protecting from migrants.

There are themes of this dichotomy, too, in the work of Italian-Ghanaian visual researcher Theophilus 'Imani' Marboah. Imani's *Echoes and Agreements* 2017–2022 photo diptych series makes powerful connections between classical imagery from Europe and the Black diaspora to interrogate how we see the other and what happens when we pair Black faces with canonical works – for instance, presenting Caravaggio's *Bacchus* c.1598 alongside a portrait of Manziga, a Chief of the Azande people in Central Africa, photographed c.1910–15 by the German zoologist Herbert Lang, who took human zoo-like images of Black Africans at the height of European colonialism on the continent. The startling symmetries in Imani's work show how the visual lens has been deployed against Black people in art history to dismiss them as undeserving of the ascription of fully embodied humanity.

In their different mediums, Imani, Alÿs and Bruguera show that art can be used to disturb embedded sociopolitical and media representations of migrants. These works show that artistic practice can counter the heavy political biases in migration coverage, helping us to pick apart how migrants

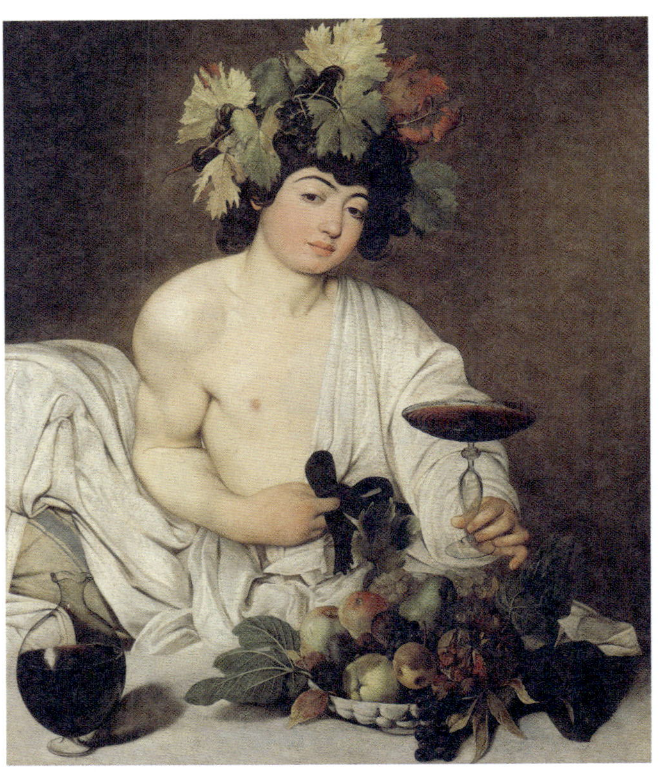

Theophilus Imani, *Echoes and Agreements* 2016—ongoing, photo
diptych project

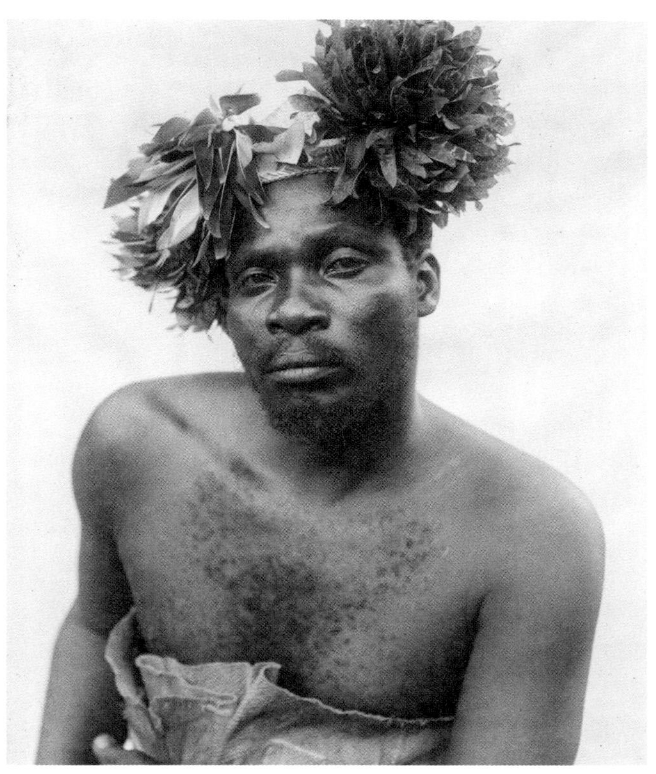

Theophilus Imani, *Echoes and Agreements* 2016–ongoing, photo diptych project

are framed socially, politically and aesthetically – framings which often work to dehumanise them. For example, the complex experiences of people on the move are too often reduced to that of unspeaking peripheral bodies. Even when migrants appear in visual documentation about them, their representation tends to be diminutive and exploitative.

'I make a home wherever I am'

By framing strangers as not 'people like us', we allow ourselves to sidestep their humanity. Vanessa Winship's work in the Balkans powerfully shows how we can genuinely humanise the depiction of refugees. In *Kukës, Albania, 1999–2002*, a group of Kosovan refugees – primarily children – stand on a hillside, staring intently in the same direction. A middle-aged man extends his arm out in an indication that is part rebuke, part petition. Around him, the children have expectant and fearful stares, but what they are staring at is out of shot.

This photograph is part of Winship's series *Imagined States and Desires: A Balkan Journey 1999–2002*, which documented the destruction of war in the Balkans. Her images show us the familiar scenes of conflict: refugee camps, people scavenging for food, convoys of people seeking safety, and the absurdity of children playing in destroyed buildings.

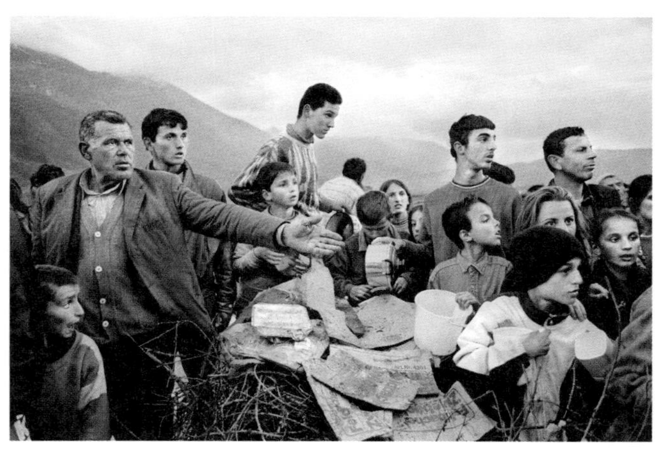

Vanessa Winship, *Kukës, Albania* 1999–2002, photograph, ink jet print on paper, 36 x 54.5, Tate

Yet, without shying away from the torment, confusion or ignominy of war, her work allows us to sit with the plight of the displaced, restoring a humanising dignity in its depiction of refugees becoming strangers to themselves.

This empathetic sentiment also shines in the work of the British-Palestinian artist Mona Hatoum. *Exodus II* 2002 comprises a pair of suitcases – one green, one yellow – connected by long strands of human hair. The work testifies to Hatoum's decades-long artistic practice of decoding the place of home and identity for those forced to flee and to live with the terrible weight of the label 'refugee'. *Exodus II* also evokes the fragility and frailty of the connection that the migrant has to home, as time and circumstance distance them from their origins. Yet the hair, the material of that remaining connection, is so redolent with biological identity and essence that its power is profound even in its near invisibility.

Another critical question is that of who gets to tell the stranger's story and how time may change the story that is told. This especially applies to those artists depicting the migrant experience from somewhere that no longer exists. Arshile Gorky's *Garden in Sochi Motif* 1942, one of three similar pieces the artist produced, speaks to how exiles depict the home they have been forced to flee, which is then destroyed. In

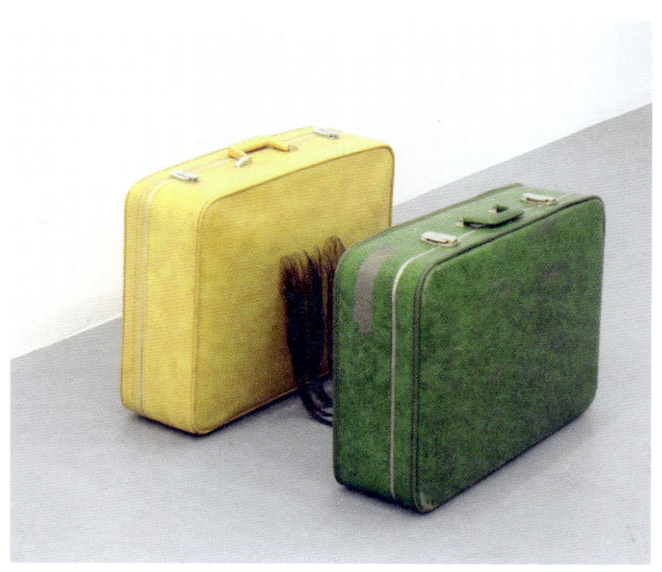

Mona Hatoum, *Exodus II* 2002, compressed card, leather, metal, human hair, Tate

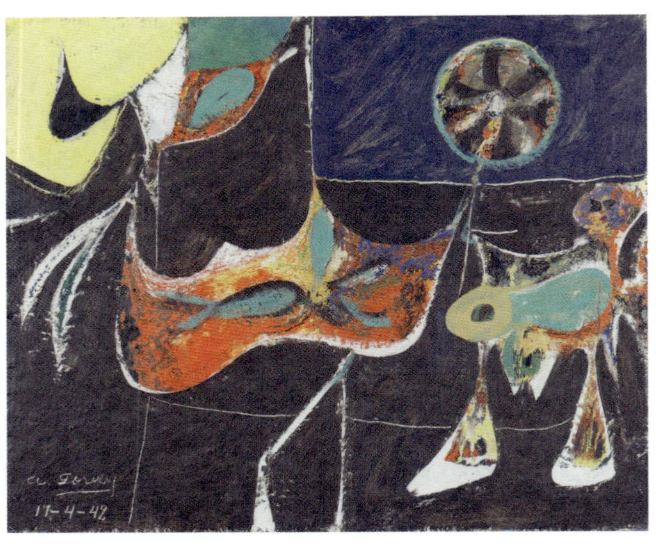

Ashile Gorky, *Garden in Sochi Motif* 1942, oil paint on canvas,
40.9 x 51, Tate

1915 Gorky fled Ottoman-controlled Armenia during the height of the genocide there. At the heart of his work is an abstract composition inspired by his childhood memories of his country – but looking at the painting today, it's almost impossible to decipher its meaning. Nonetheless, the composition of the forms, brooding black background and a smattering of radiant orange, yellow and blue colours make this a robust and alluring work. And, given the near-extinction of Armenian culture because of the genocide and the century of denial that surrounded it, Gorky's fragmented memory and fragmented style reflect a loss that is impossible to reconfigure.

Gorky eventually settled in America, where he had a foundational influence on abstract expressionism. Other strangers like him profoundly affected twentieth-century American art, among them Mark Rothko and Willem de Kooning. This was the case in Britain, too: after being held in internment camps in Scotland and the Isle of Man at the start of the Second World War, the German dadaist Kurt Schwitters lived the rest of his life in Cumbria, and his influence would shape modernism and pop art in Britain. But as Gorky found out, home and loss never leave you. The pressure on those whose job is to keep the memory alive can become unbearable. When Arshile Gorky's body was found hanging in his studio in 1948, a wooden crate nearby was inscribed with the words 'Goodbye My Loveds'.

Zarina Hashmi – known professionally as Zarina – was a Muslim-born Indian-American artist and printmaker based in New York. She is known for her longstanding practice involving drawing, woodcuts, intaglio print, and her minimalist style that evoked home, memory, and place through searing transcendental works. She once said: 'Home is the centre of my universe; I make a home wherever I am', and her work is an electrifying mesh of the personal and political.

Letters from Home 2004 comprises eight monochromatic woodblock and metal cut prints which use letters written in Urdu by the artist's sister. Zarina made printing plates from these onto handmade Kozo paper before overlaying the works on outlines of locations with particular resonance for her, such as her childhood home. In this way, 'home' goes from being a fixed place to a map of identity, moving from where the artist grew up and through the different places she has since lived and has made home not through choice but necessity. Zarina's work often circles back to the childhood home she was forced to leave by the horrors of the Pakistan-India Partition: a precise geographical location that is both real and imaginary at the same

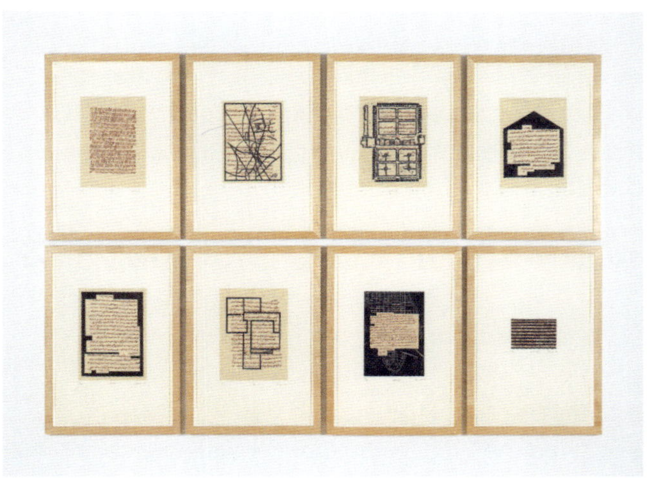

Zarina, *Letters from Home* 2004, eight metal and woodblock cut out prints on paper, each 57 x 38, Tate

time and on which she can retain a claim only through memory. For the displaced, the memory of home can be, as it is for Zarina, a sanctuary. But it can also be a prison. One cannot always be held back by the trauma of the past.

'We are over here because you were over there'

Europe's borders today are rooted in histories of empire, slavery, colonialism and extractive capitalism – sociopolitical forces that have endowed the West with ample power, wealth and dominance over countries in the Global South. The work of artist Lubaina Himid testifies to this. Himid's work examines Black representations, especially how Black women are depicted in art. In 2017 she won the Turner Prize, becoming the first Black woman to achieve this honour, recognised for her decades of work related to cultural history and her prominent role in the Black British art movement of the 1980s.

In her art practice, Himid has highlighted how ignored, forgotten or denied histories are interwoven in contemporary Britain. Himid's *H.M.S. Calcutta* 2021 references James Tissot's *The Gallery of H.M.S. Calcutta (Portsmouth)* c.1876, in the Tate Collection. While Tissot's painting depicts a flirtation between a naval officer and two young women, Himid's work

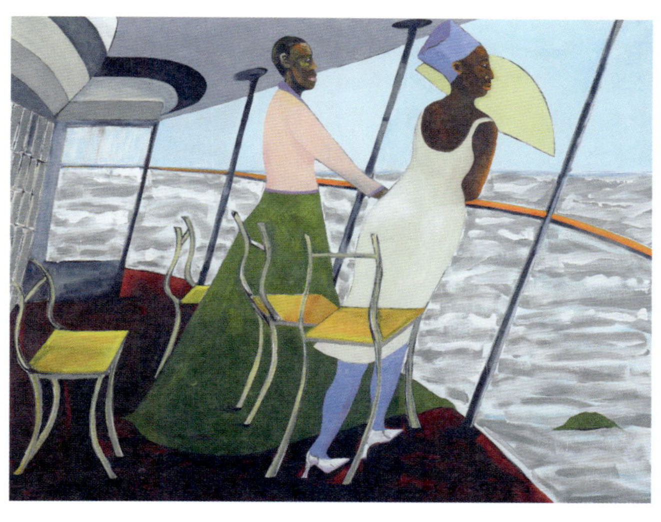

Lubaina Himid, *H.M.S. Calcutta* 2021, acrylic paint and charcoal on canvas, 183 x 244, Tate

centres on two Black women on a boat, pensively looking out at the sea before them. Himid has long dealt with the leaky borders between past and present and how depictions of Blackness fit into this. When I interviewed her in Sète in the south of France about the legacies of colonial histories in contemporary Europe and representations of migrants and refugees in the European media, Himid told me: 'I always say, "We are over here because you were over there."' This straightforward sentence is a powerful rebuttal to those who wonder why there are 'strangers' among them.

The place of the sea in migratory movements has always been crucial and terrifying. The Romans called the Mediterranean Sea 'Mare Nostrum' (Our Sea), but 'our' was never meant to include Black and Brown bodies.

Nor were these waters intended to contain the body of Scottish painter Sir David Wilkie, who died of typhoid off the coast of Gibraltar in 1841 and whose body the Governor refused to allow ashore. J.M.W. Turner painted *Peace – Burial at Sea* 1842 in Wilkie's memory, later wishing he had added more black paint to underscore the sombre sight of the body being dropped to the bottom of the sea. But even centuries on, the idea of disease and contagion exemplified by this

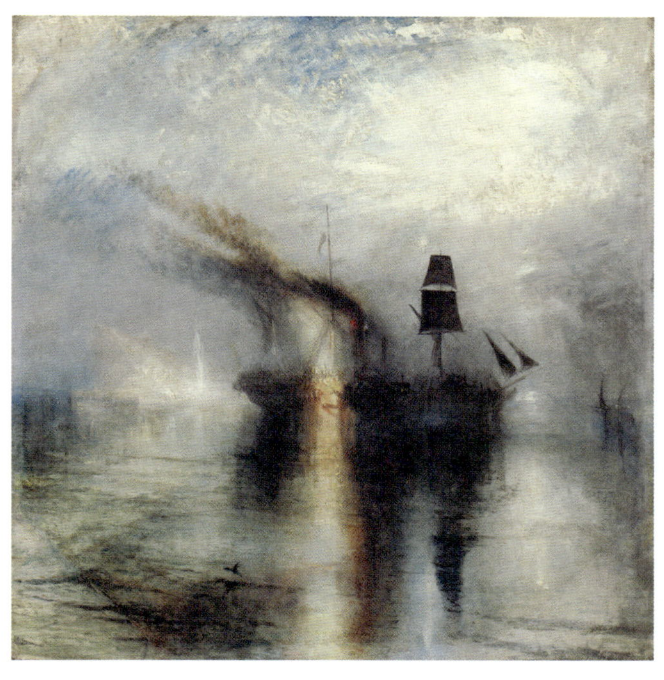

J.M.W. Turner, *Peace – Burial at Sea* 1842, oil paint on canvas,
87 x 86.7, Tate

painting has not left the Mediterranean, and Wilkie was afforded more dignity in his sea burial in 1841 than the migrants who perish today in waters that have become, in the words of Pope Francis, 'the world's largest cemetery'. Since 1993, more than 48,647 migrant deaths have been recorded in what Italian academic Alessandra di Maio, inspired by Paul Gilroy's Black Atlantic, calls the 'Black Mediterranean' – a frame to help us examine the realities at Europe's borders for the thousands of Black Africans who make the treacherous journey across these azure waters.

'The blessings are abundant!'

In early 2017, the British-Gambian artist Khadija Saye completed her photographic self-portraits series on tintypes, created using a wet collodion process developed in the nineteenth century that gives the images a historic feel, blotched and stained with black. In works such as *Peitaw* and *Nak Bejjen* from the series *Dwelling: In This Space We Breathe* 2017, Saye tackles themes of identity, spirituality and the body. That year, her work was exhibited in the Diaspora Pavilion at the Venice Biennale, besides works by Yinka Shonibare and Isaac Julien. Saye was twenty-four, and her colossal talent was finally getting the powerful recognition she so rightfully deserved: 'It's been a real journey,'

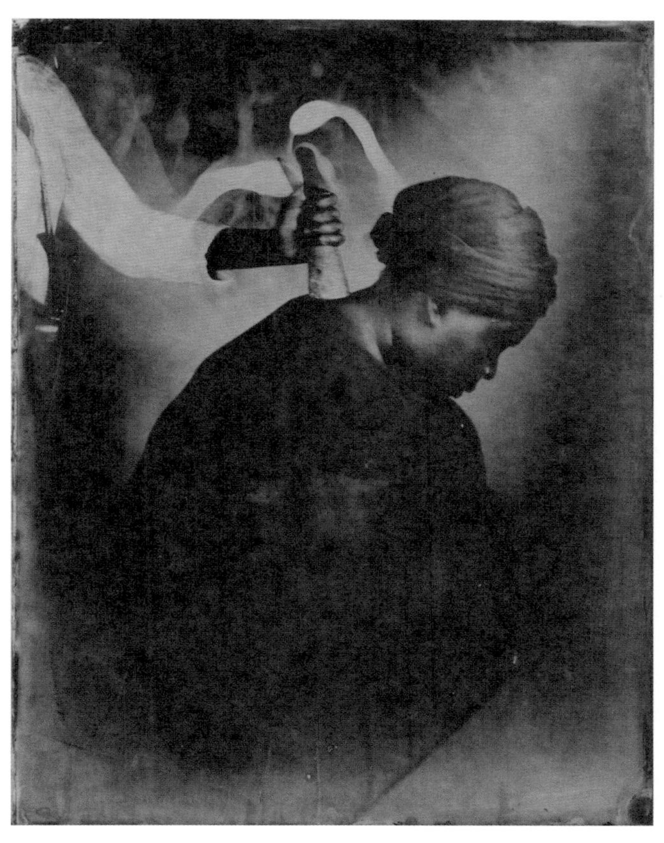

Khadija Saye, *Dwelling – In this Space we Breathe (Nak Bejjen)* 2017, tintype on metal, 25 x 20, Tate

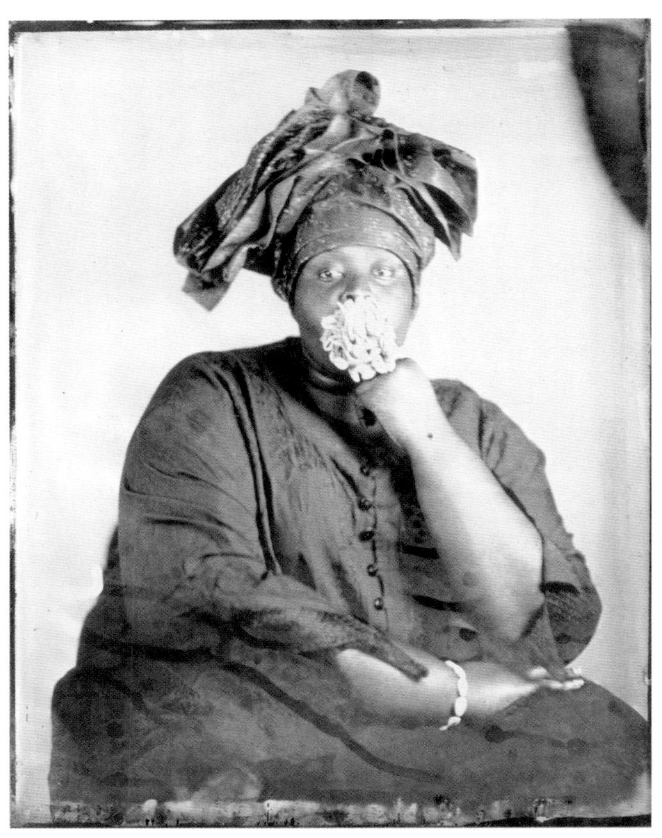

Khadija Saye, *Dwelling – In this Space we Breathe (Peitaw)* 2017, tintype on metal, 25 x 20

she tweeted from Venice, 'but mama, I'm an artist exhibiting in Venice, and the blessings are abundant!'

A month later, Saye was dead, killed in the Grenfell Tower fire. The day before she died, Saye had met an influential gallery director in London who was impressed by her work. She was within touching distance of the art career she had long dreamt of, but that dream died in an inferno that engulfed the 1970s tower in North Kensington, killing more than seventy people, including the artist and her mother.

Most residents of Grenfell Tower were of migrant backgrounds: the majority were non-white and Muslims who worked as Uber drivers, nurses, care workers and shop assistants – invisible people who lived in a tower of strangers next to pretty tree-lined Georgian homes worth millions. Their deaths brutally showcased the social divide in London, where poverty and extreme wealth rub next to each other. As so many died that June Ramadan evening, when the crescent moon hung in the sky, we were reminded of the quiet apartheid that divides many in one of the world's wealthiest cities. Six years on, there has been no accountability or justice for the victims of the Grenfell Tower fire.

Khadija Saye's life was a testament to the power of healing and transcendence. She used the best of herself and her background to create mesmerising pieces that turned the trauma of her life into bold art. She produced this work to explore the place of trauma in the Black experience and what gives us meaning and a sense of place and identity in an often-hostile world. In *Peitaw* and other works, she creates a dream-like feeling that recaptures the spirituality of African and Black diasporic identities.

Similar links are made in the work of Senegalese photographer Omar Victor Diop. In *Project Diaspora* 2014, Diop uses staged self-portraits to bring together forgotten Black people in the diaspora who lived between the fifteenth and nineteenth centuries, such as Saint Benedict the Moor, the first Black saint in history, known for his charitable works in sixteenth-century Palermo, the city of which he is a patron saint. Diop has said he chose historical figures who did not fit into the usual image frames but were 'educated, stylish and confident' – a way to sidestep the insidious white gaze on Black people and offer more nuanced and evocative comment on how historical representations of Blackness are interwoven through contemporary issues around migration and integration.

All these artworks show how we should reorient our view of strangers. In this space, art has something meaningful to say. But we also need to see that all

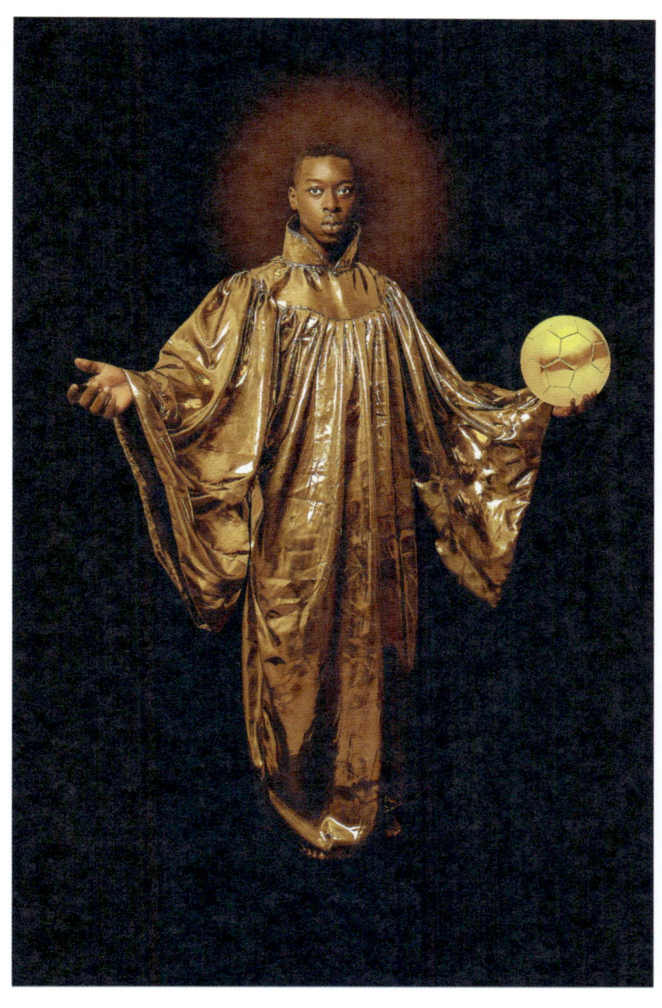

Omar Victor Diop, *St Benedicte de Palerme* (from the *Diaspora* series) 2014, inkjet print on paper, 60 x 40

strangers matter. For instance, while rightly focusing on the plight of those displaced by the brutal war in Ukraine, we have overlooked other people who have had similar experiences and face a similar fate. We have forgotten, for instance, the conflict in Ethiopia's Tigray region, where an estimated half a million people have been killed since the war began in November 2020, and millions more have been displaced. When we only see certain refugees in the media, we must question whether we see the whole picture. The danger is that we end up conceiving of 'good' versus 'bad' strangers – but people do not need to be either for them to have rights, protection and empathy. Otherwise, that line of thinking can make us view some migrants, even after generations of living somewhere, through a lens of 'strangeness'. Take, for example, the Nationality and Borders Bill of 2021 in Britain, which allows the Home Office to revoke someone's citizenship without notice. This extreme new provision, decades in the making, has reduced millions of Britons – myself included – to second-class citizens who now live in a permanent state of unease in which we remain forever strangers.

In *O the Roast Beef of Old England*, Hogarth favourably compared a prosperous and stable Britain with a France riven with pre-Revolution fever and chaos. Three centuries on, those foundations are under severe strain. Cruelty is the order of the day when it comes to keeping strangers out of our island, and our politicians appear to be infatuated with a race to the bottom on immigration. They are eroding the fundamental right to asylum and whipping up a hostile anti-migrant discourse, intending to sway voters. In this climate, we miss the humanity of the migrant to our detriment.

Where politics has failed, I wonder, is there another way through art? Can artists show us how to see the migrant beyond these negative, racialised and dehumanising frames? Art can speak to migration, integration and belonging, sparking debates and bypassing national and cultural limits to connect us. Art can also help us foster a sense of new encounter, a connection between 'us' and the 'strangers'. It's only by moving away from this problematising and dehumanising lens that we genuinely see migrants – and, in its varied forms, art as a practice can help us to sit with the plight of the stranger.

We need to use art to look and think again. The works in this book challenge us not to shy away from the pain, humanity and complexity of those on the move. They also force us to rethink how we 'see' strangers – from the ubiquitous boats and tents to the endless queues. Taken together, works by Bruguera, Winship, Hatoum, Diop, and Zarina show us the contours of the stranger's journey, and testify to the power of art to liberate the personhood of the migrant and the potential of their stories.

The final work I have chosen for this book is by the British photographer Kate Stanworth. *The Wedding* 2020 is a beautiful antidote to the images we tend to see of migrant suffering. In the photograph, a group of wedding guests – young Nigerian women dressed proudly in blue and gold – line a narrow, cobbled street in the old city of Palermo, waiting for the bride to arrive. Visible further down the street is the unassuming door to a church, previously a dwelling or simple shopfront, that now hosts congregations from the local Nigerian community for lively, rousing sermons. The wedding story is one of courage, of love over adversity: the bride and groom's relationship was the catalyst for her escape from trafficking networks and forced sexual slavery. But, of course, these wedding guests may have their own stories of hardship: leaving loved ones behind to seek a better life, trickery, disillusionment, fear and violence along the way.

For this moment, however, there is only beauty, celebration and love. And amid images of suffering and the cruel memories of forced exile, this depiction of how migrants are reshaping a changing world

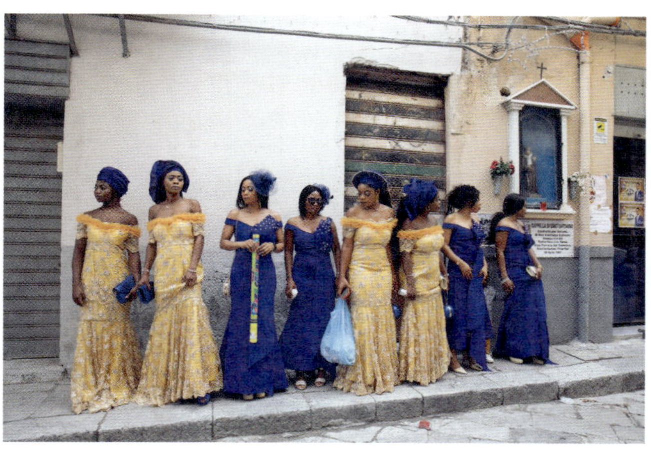

Kate Stanworth, *The Wedding* 2020, inkjet print on paper, 60 x 40

reminds me most of the Somali 'buufis' – that spirit, that air that blows and inflates the souls of migrants as they give meaning and sense to the world.